ALSO BY EDWARD HIRSCH

POETRY

*Lay Back the Darkness* (2003)

*On Love* (1998)

*Earthly Measures* (1994)

*The Night Parade* (1989)

*Wild Gratitude* (1986)

*For the Sleepwalkers* (1981)

PROSE

*Poet's Choice* (2006)

*The Demon and the Angel: Searching for the Source of Artistic Inspiration* (2002)

*Responsive Reading* (1999)

*How to Read a Poem and Fall in Love with Poetry* (1999)

EDITOR

*The Making of a Sonnet: A Norton Anthology* (2008) with Eavan Boland

*To a Nightingale: Sonnets and Poems from Sappho to Borges* (2007)

*Theodore Roethke: Selected Poems* (2005)

*William Maxwell: Memories and Appreciations* (2004) with Charles Baxter and Michael Collier

*Transforming Vision: Writers on Art* (1994)

# SPECIAL ORDERS

# SPECIAL ORDERS

*Poems*

# EDWARD HIRSCH

Alfred A. Knopf • New York • 2008

This Is a Borzoi Book Published by Alfred A. Knopf

www.aaknopf.com

Knopf, Borzoi Books, and the colophon are registered trademarks of Random House, Inc.

Library of Congress Cataloging-in-Publication Data
Hirsch, Edward.
Special orders : poems / by Edward Hirsch.— 1st ed.
p. cm.
ISBN 978-0-307-26681-1
I. Title.
PS3558.164S64 2008
811'.54—dc22      2007040336

Manufactured in the United States of America
First Edition

*For Laurie Watel*

# CONTENTS

## 1. MORE THAN HALFWAY

## 2. TO THE CLEARING

# 1. MORE THAN HALFWAY

# Special Orders

Give me back my father walking the halls
   of Wertheimer Box and Paper Company
      with sawdust clinging to his shoes.

Give me back his tape measure and his keys,
   his drafting pencil and his order forms;
      give me his daydreams on lined paper.

I don't understand this uncontainable grief.
   Whatever you had that never fit,
      whatever else you needed, believe me,

my father, who wanted your business,
   would squat down at your side
      and sketch you a container for it.

# Cotton Candy

We walked on the bridge over the Chicago River
for what turned out to be the last time,
and I ate cotton candy, that sugary air,
that sweet blue light spun out of nothingness.
It was just a moment, really, nothing more,
but I remember marveling at the sturdy cables
of the bridge that held us up
and threading my fingers through the long
and slender fingers of my grandfather,
an old man from the Old World
who long ago disappeared into the nether regions.
And I remember that eight-year-old boy
who had tasted the sweetness of air,
which still clings to my mouth
and disappears when I breathe.

# Branch Library

I wish I could find that skinny, long-beaked boy
who perched in the branches of the old branch library.

He spent the Sabbath flying between the wobbly stacks
and the flimsy wooden tables on the second floor,

pecking at nuts, nesting in broken spines, scratching
notes under his own corner patch of sky.

I'd give anything to find that birdy boy again
bursting out into the dusky blue afternoon

with his satchel of scrawls and scribbles,
radiating heat, singing with joy.

# Playing the Odds

The Vegas lights are glaring at one a.m.
and I can still see my bulky first father
standing at the craps table
whispering softly to the dice,
*Come on, baby, come home to Daddy.*

He is surrounded by strangers who are
shouting out numbers, laying down bets,
and he is massively alone, like God
playing dice with the universe
on a felt table in a fake city.

My sister and I watch him from the crowd.
Our father wants a seven coming out.
He wants to roll dice until he can't win
anymore, and then he needs to lose.
But everyone likes him for that seven.

I was two years old when I last saw him
blowing on the dice in our kitchen.
*These are the true numbers,* he said,
cupping them in his palms,
and then he tossed them on the table.

I remember the sweaty warmth
of those dice before he threw them.
I wonder if God Himself
breathed into the nostrils of His son
with as much tenderness and desperation.

*—for Harold Rubenstein, 1928–2004*

# My Father's Track-and-Field Medal, 1932

Cup the tarnished metal in your palm.
Look closely and you'll see a squirrel
scampering up a beech-wood in the forest.
You'll see a cardinal flaming in the branches.
You'll see a fleet-footed antelope racing
through the woods ahead of the hunters.

# Cold Calls

If you had watched my father,
who had been peddling boxes for fifty years,
working the phones again at a common desk,

if you had listened to him sweet-talking
the newly minted assistant buyer at Seagram's

and swearing a little under his breath,

if you had sweated with him on the docks
of a medical supply company
and heard him boasting, as I did,
that he had to kiss some strange asses,

if you had seen him dying out there,

then you would understand why I stood
at his grave on those wintry afternoons
and stared at the bare muddy trees

and raved in silence to no one,
to his name carved into a granite slab.

Cold calls, dead accounts.

# Second-Story Warehouse

SUMMER 1966

Come with me to the second-story warehouse
    where I filled orders for the factory downstairs,
and commanded the freight elevator, and read
    high in the air on a floating carpet of boxes.

I could touch the damp pipes in the ceiling
    and smell the rust. I could look over
the Puerto Rican workers in the parking lot,
    smoking and laughing and kidding around

in Spanish during their break, especially Julia,
    who bit my lower lip until it bruised and bled,
and taught me to roll cigarettes in another language,
    and called me her virgin boy from the suburbs.

All summer I read Neruda's *Canto General*
    and took lessons from Juan, who trained me
to accept orders with dignity—*dignidad*—
    and never take any shit from the foreman.

He showed off the iron plate in his skull
    from a bar fight with a drunken supervisor,
while the phone blinked endlessly from Shipping
    & Handling, and light glinted off the forklift.

I felt like a piece of wavy, fluted paper
    trapped between two sheets of linerboard
in the single wall, double-faced boxes
    we lifted and cursed, sweated and stacked

on top of heavy wooden skids. I dreaded
    the large, unwieldy industrial A-flutes
and the 565 stock cartons that we carried
    in bundles through the dusty aisles

while downstairs a line of blue collars fed
    slotting, gluing, and stitching machines.
Juan taught me about mailers and multidepths
    and praised the torrential rains of childhood,

the oysters that hid in the bloody coral,
    their pearls shimmering in the twisted rock,
green stones polished by furious storms
    and coconut palms waving in the twilight.

He praised the sun that floats over the island
    like a bell ringed with fire, or a sea rose,
and the secret torch that forever burns
    inside us, a beacon no one can touch.

Come with me to the second-story warehouse
   where I learned the difference between
RSC, FOL, die-cuts, and five-panel folders,
   and saw the iron shine inside a skull.

Every day at precisely three in the afternoon
   we delivered our orders to the loading dock.
*We may go down dusty and tired,* Juan said,
   *but we come back smelling like the sea.*

# The Swimmers

*—for Gerald Stern*


We warbled on the muddy banks
and waded up to our throats in the Delaware River,

talking about Ovid washing himself in the Black Sea
and Paul Celan floating face-down in the Seine.

We swam arm over arm through the green silt
and coasted along on our backs, marveling and mourning

for Shelley drowning off the shore at Viareggio
and Li Po tumbling drunkenly into the Yangtze.

These were the strokes we praised, weren't they,
the butterfly and the crawl, the lullabies

we crooned on the first warm day of summer
in honor of the non-swimmers Crane and Berryman,

in honor of Orpheus, whose butchered head
is forever singing above the choppy waves.

# The Chardin Exhibition

*—for William Maxwell*

While I was studying the copper cistern
and the silver goblet, a soup tureen
with a cat stalking a partridge and hare,

you were gulping down the morning light
and moving from the bedstand to the bureau,
from the shuttered window to the open door.

While I was taking my time over a pristine jar
of apricots and a basket of wild strawberries—
a pyramid leaning toward a faceted glass—

you were sitting at a low breakfast table
eating a soft-boiled egg—just one—
from a tiny, hesitant, glittering spoon.

While I was absorbed in a duck hanging
by one leg and a hare with a powder flask
and a game bag, which you wanted me to see,

you were lying on the living room couch
for a nap, one of your last, next to
a white porcelain vase with two carnations.

I wish I could have stood there with you
in front of Chardin's last self-portrait,
exclaiming over his turban with a bow

and the red splash of his pastel crayon—
a new medium—which he used, dearest,
to defy death on a sheet of blue paper.

# On the Rhine

*—in memory of Rose Ausländer, 1901–1988*

I couldn't find the Nelly Sachs Home
    for the Jewish elderly in Düsseldorf
where I wanted to bring flowers
    to the roseland of her final room,

and so I wandered into an empty garden
    with a basket of wild strawberries
and a loaf of coarse country bread, as if
    I were living in a Goethe poem,

and sat under the catalpas and lindens
    that drive you mad with their sweetness
so that you want to forget everything,

and listened to the little European nightingale
    singing amidst our homelessness
as if the twentieth century had never happened.

# Kraków, 6 A.M.

*—for Adam Zagajewski*

I sit in a corner of the town square
and let the ancient city move through me.
I sip a cup of coffee, write a little,
and watch an old woman sweeping the stairs.

Poland is waking up now: blackbirds patrol
the cobblestones, nuns rush by in habits,
and the clock tower strikes six times.
Day breaks into the night's reverie.

The morning is as fresh and clean
as a butcher's apron hanging in a shop.
Now it is pressed and white, but soon
it will be spotted with blood.

Europe is waking up, but America
is going to sleep, a gangly teenager
sprawled out on a comfortable bed.
He has large hands and feet

and his dreams are innocent and bloodthirsty.
I want to throw a blanket over his shoulders
and tuck him in again, like a child,
now that his sleep is no longer untroubled.

I'm alone here in the Old World
where poetry matters, old hatreds seethe,

and history wears a crown of thorns.
Fresh bread wafts from the ovens

and daily life follows its own inexorable
course, like a drunk weaving slowly
across a courtyard, or a Dutch maid
throwing open the heavy shutters.

I suppose there's always a shopgirl
stationed in the doorway, a beggar taking up
his corner post, and newspapers fluttering
from store to store with bad news.

Poetry, too, seeks a place in the world—
feasting on darkness but needing light,
taking confession, listening for bells,
for the first strains of music in a town square.

Europe is going to work now—
look at those two businessmen hurrying
past the statue of the national bard—
as her younger brother sleeps

on the other side of the ocean,
innocent and violent, dreaming of glory.

# Elegy for the Jewish Villages

*—after Antoni Słonimsky*

The Jewish villages in Poland are gone now—
Hrubieszów, Karczew, Brody, Falenica . . .
There are no Sabbath candles lit in the windows,
no chanting comes from the wooden synagogues.

The Jewish villages in Poland have vanished
and so I walked through a graveyard without graves.
It must have been hard work to clean up after the war:
someone must have sprinkled sand over the blood,
swept away the footprints, and whitewashed the walls
with bluish lime. Someone must have fumigated
the streets, the way you do after a plague.

One moon glitters here—cold, pale, alien.
I stood in the dark countryside in summer but
could never find the two golden moons of Chagall
glittering outside the town when the night lights up.
Those moons are orbiting another planet now.

Gone are the towns where the shoemaker was a poet,
the watchmaker a philosopher, the barber a troubadour.

Gone are the villages where the wind joined biblical songs
with Polish tunes, where old Jews stood in the shade
of cherry trees and longed for the holy walls of Jerusalem.

Gone now are the hamlets that passed away
like a shadow that falls between our words.

I am bringing you home the story of a world—
Hrubieszów, Karczew, Brody, Falenica . . .
Come close and listen to this song—
the Jewish villages in Poland are gone now—
from another one of the saddest nations on earth.

# Soutine: A Show
# of Still Lifes

It started with herrings, which he ate
with warm black bread as a child,
and ended with two pigs, the forbidden.

It started with the strict dietary laws
of his father, a pious Jew, a mender,
and ended with ulcers, which he disobeyed.

He was snubbed by a bouquet
of colorful flowers on a balcony
and a pretty pink vase with flowers,

but red gladiolas from the countryside
in a flower shop next to a laundry
suddenly reached out to him.

He never expected so much water
in a dead rayfish, so much fire
in a turkey hanging from a fireplace.

He never expected to find his soul
hiding in a chicken splayed
open-winged on the blue ground.

Who needed a mirror against the wall?
He found an enormous carcass of beef
with all of its entrails exposed.

He loved the savagery of the match
and slashed his brush into the canvas
until the painting wobbled on its legs.

He was a boxer forcing his opponent
into a tight corner, taking him apart
with quick jabs and a right cross.

One punch for a shack in Smilovitchi,
two punches for a pair of older brothers
who attacked him in the kitchen.

One punch for the village thug
who thrashed him for drawing a rabbi,
two punches for the Second Commandment.

"Thou shalt not . . ." But Rembrandt painted
the portrait of a bearded Jew, a woman
bathing in a stream, the slaughtered ox.

Homage to the Jewish painters in Paris:
a scrawny hen for Kikoïne, a donkey
for Chagall, a pheasant for Modigliani.

He traveled back and forth to the Louvre.
He carried a giant slab of meat
on his back through the graveyard.

His lover said that his studio looked
like a slaughterhouse on Friday afternoon.
He no longer kept the Sabbath,

but he could scarcely endure the stench
and sprinkled blood on the carcass
to keep it fresh, like an open wound.

Some days his brush was a knife,
some days a scalpel. Some days
he worked like a surgeon

separating the ligaments of a patient
wounded on the table, calmly
cutting the flesh away from the bone.

He could not forget the village butcher
who shouted out with joy
when he sliced the neck of a bird

and drained the force out of it.
He could not abandon the boy
who had stifled his cry.

Let's leave a space for the paintings
that he lacerated and destroyed
with the radical fury of the creator.

Let's leave a space for his portraits
of the wind in the French countryside,
invisible presences, awe-filled nights.

It was a calm day. A void encircled
a solitary figure of flayed beef.
A void enclosed the painter.

I stood in the middle of a silent room
and surveyed the beauty of carnage,
the dangerous carnage of beauty.

So many brushstrokes in a painting,
and so much blood. So much art
in a still life, and so much death.

# The Minimalist Museum

I am driving past our house on Sul Ross
across the street from the minimalist museum.

I am looking up at the second-story window
where I gazed down at the curators

carrying their leather satchels to work
and the schoolchildren gathering on the front lawn.

I spent my forties at that window, stirring milk
into my coffee and brooding about the past,

listening to Satie's experiments and Cage's
dicey music wafting over the temple of modernism.

I chanced a decade at that window, impervious
to the precarious moment, the broken moon-

light flooding over the neighborhood trees,
my wife's moody insomnia, my son's fitful sleep,

and sacrificing another five years, another ten years,
to the minor triumphs, the major failures.

# Self-portrait

I lived between my heart and my head,
like a married couple who can't get along.

I lived between my left arm, which is swift
and sinister, and my right, which is righteous.

I lived between a laugh and a scowl,
and voted against myself, a two-party system.

My left leg dawdled or danced along,
my right cleaved to the straight and narrow.

My left shoulder was like a stripper on vacation,
my right stood upright as a Roman soldier.

Let's just say that my left side was the organ
donor and leave my private parts alone,

but as for my eyes, which are two shades
of brown, well, Dionysus, meet Apollo.

Look at Eve raising her left eyebrow
while Adam puts his right foot down.

No one expected it to survive,
but divorce seemed out of the question.

I suppose my left hand and my right hand
will be clasped over my chest in the coffin

and I'll be reconciled at last,
I'll be whole again.

# A Few Encounters
## with My Face

### 1

Who is that moonlit stranger staring at me
through the fog of a bathroom mirror

### 2

Wrinkles form a parenthesis around the eyes
dry wells of sadness at three a.m.

### 3

The forehead furrows in a scowl
a question mark puzzled since childhood

### 4

Faint scrawl of chicken pox and measles
broken asthma nights breathing steam

### 5

Hair thinning like his grandfather's
all those bald ancestral thoughts

### 6

The nose a ram's horn a scroll
as long and bumpy as the centuries

### 7

Greed of a Latvian horse thief
surprised by the lights

8

Primitive double chin divided in two
a mother and father divorcing


9

Deep red pouches and black bags
a life given to sleeplessness


1 0

Earnest grooves ironic blotches secret scars
memories medallions of middle age


1 1

It would take a Cubist to paint
this dark face splitting in three directions


1 2

Identify these features with rapture and despair
one part hilarity two parts grief

# Man Without a Face

I fell asleep at the wooden desk
and when I woke up startled
in the wintry light—
I can't explain this—
my face stayed in my hands.

I tried to wash my thoughts
in icy water over the sink,
but when I looked up
the mirror had become a blank
white wall, wrinkled and creased.

Now I am a man walking around
without a face to compose,
a skeleton, a stranger to myself,
an aching bone, a nerve exposed.

# To My Shadow

You stand behind me at the podium,
a mute accuser, and refuse to speak.
Words mean nothing to you.

Later, you rush ahead of me
on a deserted street, a total stranger,
while I hurry to catch up to you.

You have the floating liquidity of
a ghost who disappears around corners
and takes on odd shapes in the dark.

Sometimes you cling to me, a shady
figure slouching in doorways and alleys,
but other times you vanish completely.

Shadowy self, lonely double, I don't know
which of us is more insubstantial.

# More Than Halfway

I've turned on lights all over the house,
but nothing can save me from this darkness.

I've stepped onto the front porch to see
the stars perforating the milky black clouds

and the moon staring coldly through the trees,
but this negative I'm carrying inside me.

Where is the boy who memorized constellations?
What is the textbook that so consoled him?

I'm now more than halfway to the grave,
but I'm not half the man I meant to become.

To what fractured deity can I pray?
I'm willing to pay the night with interest,

though the night wants nothing but itself.
What did I mean to say to darkness?

Death is a zero hollowed out of my chest.
God is an absence whispering in the leaves.

# A Partial History
# of My Stupidity

Traffic was heavy coming off the bridge,
and I took the road to the right, the wrong one,
and got stuck in the car for hours.

Most nights I rushed out into the evening
without paying attention to the trees,
whose names I didn't know,
or the birds, which flew heedlessly on.

I couldn't relinquish my desires
or accept them, and so I strolled along
like a tiger that wanted to spring
but was still afraid of the wildness within.

The iron bars seemed invisible to others,
but I carried a cage around inside me.

I cared too much what other people thought
and made remarks I shouldn't have made.
I was silent when I should have spoken.

Forgive me, philosophers,
I read the Stoics but never understood them.

I felt that I was living the wrong life,
spiritually speaking,
while halfway around the world

thousands of people were being slaughtered,
some of them by my countrymen.

So I walked on—distracted, lost in thought—
and forgot to attend to those who suffered
far away, nearby.

Forgive me, faith, for never having any.

I did not believe in God,
who eluded me.

# 2. TO THE CLEARING

# Late March

Saturday morning in late March.
I was alone and took a long walk,
though I also carried a book
of the Alone, which companioned me.

The day was clear, unnaturally clear,
like a freshly wiped pane of glass,
a window over the water,
and blue, preternaturally blue,
like the sky in a Magritte painting,
and cold, vividly cold, so that
you could clap your hands and remember
winter, which had left a few moments ago—
if you strained, you could almost see it
disappearing over the hills in a black parka.
Spring was coming but hadn't arrived yet.
I walked on the edge of the park.
The wind whispered a secret to the trees,
which held their breath
and scarcely moved.
On the other side of the street,
the skyscrapers stood on tiptoe.

I walked down to the pier to watch
the launching of a passenger ship.
Ice had broken up on the river
and the water rippled smoothly in blue light.
The moon was a faint smudge

in the clouds, a brushstroke, an afterthought
in the vacant mind of the sky.
Seagulls materialized out of vapor
amidst the masts and flags.
*Don't let our voices die on land,*
they cawed, swooping down for fish
and then soaring back upwards.

The kiosks were opening
and couples moved slowly past them,
arm in arm, festive.
Children darted in and out of walkways,
which sprouted with vendors.
Voices cut the air.
Kites and balloons. Handmade signs.
Voyages to unknown places.
The whole day had the drama of an expectation.

Down at the water, the queenly ship
started moving away from the pier.
Banners fluttered.
The passengers clustered at the rails on deck.
I stood with the people onshore and waved
goodbye to the travelers.
Some were jubilant;
others were brokenhearted.
I have always been both.

Suddenly, a great cry went up.
The ship set sail for the horizon
and rumbled into the future,

but the cry persisted
and cut the air
like an iron bell ringing
in an empty church.
I looked around the pier,
but everyone else was gone
and I was left alone
to peer into the ghostly distance.
I had no idea where that ship was going,
but I felt lucky to see it off
and bereft when it disappeared.

# Green Night

We walked down the path to breakfast.
The morning swung open like an iron gate.

We sat in Adirondack chairs and argued
for hours about the self—it wasn't personal—

and the nature of nature, the broken
Word, the verse of God in fragments.

We trotted back and forth to readings.
The trees were the greenest I had ever seen.

We cut bread from a large brown loaf
at a long wooden table in the mountains.

A farmer hayed the meadows
and the afternoon flared around us.

Pass the smoky flask. Pass the cigarettes:
twenty smoldering friends in a package.

We swam in the muddy pond at dusk.
The sky was a purple I had never seen.

Someone was always hungover,
scheming with rhymes, hanging out.

Nothing could quench our thirst for each other.
At the bonfire, we flamed with words.

The houses were named after trees.
I slept with someone at the top of a maple.

It was a green night to be a poet in those days.
We didn't care if the country didn't care about us.

# To D. B.

I miss your apartment on West Eleventh Street
where I slept off the front hall in a bedroom
that would have been a closet in another city.

The plants breathed easily in their heavy pots,
but the radiators knocked all night, like ghosts
trying to reach us from the other side.

The traffic on Sixth Avenue was a slow buzz.
Someone rattled a dog chain in the moonlight
that bathed the schoolyard across the street.

Light seeped in through the barred windows.
I could hear Faith rustling around downstairs,
getting ready for work, unwilling to die.

If there is a West Village in the other world,
we will someday meet there. I'll reach over
and hug you, which will make you uneasy.

Let's go for a bottle of wine at the tavern
near the branch library and then stroll over
to Citarella for prosciutto and melon.

You can buy a pack of cigarettes at the corner
and explain the architecture to me. Maybe
I can stay at your place until I get settled.

# Bounty

*—for Daniel Stern, 1928–2007*

You had your compass, your city campus,
your briefcase crammed with stories.
(Your case for the writer was brief: guilty.)

You had your novels and twice-told tales,
and cruised down the stairs like Bartleby
in reverse: a scrivener who preferred to.

You had your Franz Kafka and Max Brod,
the jackdaw and the man of letters
laughing their heads off on a corner in Prague.

You had the Jewish past in Budapest,
the hunger of dying, the Hungarian dead,
grief-stricken music for violin and cello.

You had your hardships and holidays,
your high holy days, your nights of mourning
and your days of awe, your celebrations.

You had your car rides careening around corners,
and when you walked, you were never pedestrian.
You had your Gloria, your Book of Daniel;
you had your own stern covenant with life.

# To Houston

My brash, impolitic, overdeveloped city,
my oil-stained country of three seasons
(you never pretended to have a winter),

my gonzo younger brother who looks stiff
in a white collar (who can blame him?)
and made a fortune selling futures,

my older sister who wears too much makeup
and still looks smart in a pantsuit
(how many times has she been married?),

my mixed neighborhood of Mexican immigrants
and modernist temples (the Menil, the Rothko),
my mystic nights of poetry, oh Houston,

after eighteen years of trying to embrace
your theatrical storms and unforgiving heat,
high ozone, no zoning, strip malls, strip clubs,

I drove away from you on a scorched afternoon
in late summer and haven't looked back since
at your long steaming ribbons of asphalt.

You swell like music in my memory.
I raised a son in you—or tried to—and buried
more than my dead in your baked earth.

# Eighteen Steps

That was the winter of the broken foot
and the new position, the misery

of hobbling down eighteen steps onto the open ground
and then passing through the filthy turnstile

and the fetid tunnel, like the other sinners, suits
and ties crowding onto one train after another

that clattered shut and whisked away, depositing us
on the other side, delivering us to the platform

and the crumbling stairs, to the iron railing
where I dragged myself out of the earth

and faced a crippled trumpeter
on the corner, my twin,

my job,
the endless gleaming buildings.

# Charades

We waited on two sides of the subway tracks:
you were riding uptown and I was heading downtown
to a different apartment, after all these years.

We were almost paralyzed, as anxious
travelers surged around us in waves,
and then you started to pantomime.

First you touched your right eye.
Then you palmed your left knee.
Finally, you pointed at me.

I made a sign of understanding
back to you, but the train suddenly roared
into the station and you disappeared.

# Boy with a Headset

He is wearing baggy shorts and a loud T-shirt
and singing along to his headset on Broadway.
Every now and then he glances back at me,
a middle-aged father weaving through traffic behind him.

He is a fifteen-year-old in the city—no more, no less—
but I imagine him as a colorful unnamed bird
warbling his difference from the robins and sparrows
and scissoring past the vendors on every corner.

I keep thinking of him as a wild fledgling
who tilts precariously on one wing
and peers back at me from the sudden height
before sailing out over the treetops.

# Green Figs

I want to live like that little fig tree
    that sprouted up at the beach last spring
        and spread its leaves over the sandy rock.

All summer its stubborn green fruit
    (tiny flowers covered with a soft skin)
        ripened and grew in the bright salt spray.

The Tree of the Knowledge of Good
    and Evil was a fig tree, or so it is said,
        but this wild figure was a wanton stray.

I need to live like that crooked tree—
    solitary, bittersweet, and utterly free—
        that knelt down in the hardest winds

but could not be blasted away.
    It kept its eye on the far horizon
        and brought honey out of the rock.

# The Sweetness

*Tornami avanti, s'alcun dolce mai ebbe 'l cor tristo . . .*
—PETRARCH, #272

The times my sad heart knew a little sweetness
come back to me now: the coffee shop
in Decatur, the waffle house in Macon . . .

The highway signs pointed to our happiness;
the greasy spoons and gleaming truck stops
were the stations of our pilgrimage.

Remember the flock of Baptist women flying
off the bus and gathering on the bridge
over the river, singing with praise?

Wasn't that us staggering past the riverboats,
eating homemade fudge at the county fair
and devouring each other's body?

They come back to me now, delicious love,
the times my sad heart knew a little sweetness.

# To Lethargy

You were like a steady low-grade fever,
a dull relative from Rochester,
a cloudy gray sky in late November.

He thought of you as the middle daughter
of boredom and the sister of torpor,
a close second cousin to fear.

Listlessness, you were a passive aggressor
who sat on his chest by the hour
and oppressed him by the year.

Acedia, couch potato, sluggish philosopher,
you shone on him like a dead star
and suckled him on the breast of despair.

But one day he walked away from you, dear,
and never looked back from the top stair.

# Gnostic Gospels

We are like a surviving Gnostic sect,
   living in caves and eating fallen fruit,
      practicing our own brand of adoration

which is devoted to wondrous signs,
   inner mysteries, the radical unknown.
      *If you bring forth what is within you,*

*what you bring forth will save you.*
   *If you do not bring forth what is within you,*
      *what you do not bring forth will destroy you,*

so Jesus said. Let others praise
   the electrifying force of mass media,
      or kneel at the bruised altar of politics.

We keep faith with the technology
   of the body, with the voices of pilgrims
      naming the unnamed and resurrecting

dead languages of grief, inaudible pitches
   of praise. We believe in the root power
      of words, dreams, ecstatic trances, visions.

*You are my twin and true companion,*
    Jesus said to the citizen, *examine yourself*
        *and be called "the one who knows himself."*

It's true that our robes were stripped
    from us, yet we are as stubborn as birds
        searching for morsels of food in winter.

# A New Theology

God couldn't bear their happiness
when He heard them laughing together in the garden.
He caught them kneeling down in the dirt
(or worse) and letting pomegranate juice
run down their faces. He found them
breaking open a fig with fresh delight
as if something crucial had dawned upon them.
I think the whole shebang—the serpent, the apple
with knowledge of good and evil—was a setup
because God couldn't stand being alone
with His own creation, while Adam and Eve celebrated
as a man and a woman together in Paradise,
exactly like us, love, exactly like us.

# Happiness Writes White

I am a piece of chalk
scrawling words on an empty blackboard.

I am a banner of smoke
that crosses the blue air and doesn't dissolve.

I don't believe that only sorrow
and misery can be written.

Happiness, too, can be precise:

Doctor, there's a keen throbbing
on the left side of my chest
where my ribs are wrenched by joy.

Wings flutter in my shoulders
and blood courses through my body
like waves cresting on a choppy sea.

Look: the eyes blur with tears
and the tears clear.

My head is like skylight.
My heart is like dawn.

# I Wish I Could Paint You

I wish I could paint you—
your lanky body, lithe, coltish, direct.
I need a brush for your hard angles
and ferocious blues and reds.
I need to stretch a fresh canvas
to catch you stretched across the bed.

I wish I could paint you
from the waist up—your gangling arms
and flat chest, your long neck
(it would take Modigliani to capture it)
that has caused you so much pain
holding up your proud head.

I wish I could paint you
from the waist down—your cheeky
ass, your cunt like the steely eye
of a warrior queen, your tall
thoroughbred legs—headlong, furious—
that have ridden me to victory.

I watch you sleeping next to me
in a patch of light, or stepping out
of the shower in the early morning,
your smile as wide as the sea
and your eyes that are deeper blue.
I wish I could paint you.

# To the Subway

Underground horse, I board you at Grand Central
and ride your steely body away from the city
with the other riders, the collared and collarless.

I prefer you expressly, at off-hours,
but I hang from your bars at peak times
and sway to your snorting music.

I lean in to your turns in dank tunnels
and hurtle with you through the darkness
for long stretches, between fitful stops.

I'm not pretending I never curse you
for rearing up between stations, breaking down
on Thursdays, or resting in your stable,

and yet you carry me faithfully to Atlantic
where I step across the gap onto firm shore
and climb your stairs into the bright air.

# As I Walked Home
# from the Hospital

it was a blistering hot
Sunday morning in mid-July;
the sun throbbed like a headache
in the skull of the sky.

It was bright too, too bright
to look at the barred windows
and sunburnt foreheads
of the towering shadows.

I walked the deserted streets—
every street was a search—
until I heard a gospel choir
singing by a locked church.

The black-robed jubilee
sweltered and swayed
and praised the hour
earth was made.

And I was glad to be outside
on this scathing day
when nothing could stop
my relentless joy.

# Green Couch

That was the year I lived without fiction
and slept surrounded by books on the unconscious.
I woke every morning to a sturdy brown oak.

That was the year I left behind my marriage
of twenty-eight years, my faded philosophy books, and
the green couch I had inherited from my grandmother.

After she died, I drove it across the country
and carried it up three flights of crooked stairs
to a tiny apartment in West Philadelphia,

and stored it in my in-laws' basement in Bethesda,
and left it to molder in our garage in Detroit
(my friend Dennis rescued it for his living room),

and moved it to a second-floor study in Houston
and a fifth-floor apartment on the Upper West Side,
where it will now be carted away to the dump.

All my difficult reading took place on that couch,
which was turning back into the color of nature
while I grappled with ethics and the law,

the reasons for Reason, Being and Nothingness,
existential dread and the death of God
(I'm still angry at Him for no longer existing).

That was the year when I finally mourned
for my two dead fathers, my sole marriage,
and the electric green couch of my past.

Darlings, I remember everything.
But now I try to speak the language of
the unconscious and study earth for secrets.

I go back and forth to work.
I walk in the botanical gardens on weekends
and take a narrow green path to the clearing.

# A Night in September

I have traveled hundreds of miles
to spread my sleeping bag in this empty field.

I have watched a crescent floating overhead,
a wooden cradle on the river.

I have left the war-torn terror of the city
to listen to the wind soothing the grass

on a crisp night in September
in a new century.

I have traveled so far
for a fleeting moment of peace

in starlit sleep,
charmed, beckoning . . .

The ground pillows my head,
the sky blankets me.

# After a Long
# Insomniac Night

I walked down to the sea in the early morning
after a long insomniac night.

I climbed over the giant gull-colored rocks
and moved past the trees,
tall dancers stretching their limbs
and warming up in the blue light.

I entered the salty water, a penitent
whose body was stained,
and swam toward a red star rising
in the east—regal, purple-robed.

One shore disappeared behind me
and another beckoned.
                          I confess
that I forgot the person I had been
as easily as the clouds drifting overhead.

My hands parted the water.
The wind pressed at my back, wings
and my soul floated over the whitecapped waves.

ACKNOWLEDGMENTS

"Special Orders," "My Father's Track-and-Field Medal, 1932," and "Cold Calls" are dedicated to Kurt Hirsch (1913–2002).

Special thanks to the editors of the following publications where these poems, some of which have been revised, first appeared:

*A Book for Daniel Stern, Gulf Coast:* "Bounty"

*Alaska Quarterly Review:* "Happiness Writes White"

*The American Poetry Review:* "Cotton Candy," "Playing the Odds," "Man Without a Face," "To My Shadow," "A New Theology," "I Wish I Could Paint You," "After a Long Insomniac Night"

*Five Points:* "My Father's Track-and-Field Medal, 1932," "Elegy for the Jewish Villages," "Kraków, 6 A.M."

*The Hopkins Review:* "The Sweetness"

*Image:* "More Than Halfway," under the title "Poem at 45"

*McSweeney's:* "To D.B."

*The New Republic:* "Cold Calls"

*The New Yorker:* "The Chardin Exhibition," "Self-portrait," "Boy with a Headset," and "A Partial History of My Stupidity"

*The New York Review of Books:* "Special Orders"

*The New York Times:* "Green Figs"

*The Paris Review:* "On the Rhine," "Green Night"

*Per Contra:* "The Minimalist Museum"

*Ploughshares:* "Soutine: A Show of Still Lifes"

*Poetry:* "Branch Library," "The Swimmers," "Late March"

*Rattapallax:* "Second-Story Warehouse"

*Slate:* "Gnostic Gospels," "Green Couch"

*The Threepenny Review:* "To the Subway"

*TriQuarterly:* "A Few Encounters with My Face"

## A Note About the Author

Edward Hirsch is the author of six previous collections of poetry, including *Wild Gratitude,* which won the National Book Critics Circle Award, and *Lay Back the Darkness*. He has also published four prose books, among them *How to Read a Poem and Fall in Love with Poetry,* a national best seller. He has received numerous awards for his poetry, including a MacArthur Fellowship, and publishes regularly in a wide variety of magazines and journals, such as *The American Poetry Review* and *The New Yorker*. A longtime teacher in the creative writing program at the University of Houston, he is now the president of the John Simon Guggenheim Memorial Foundation.

## A Note on the Type

The text of this book was set in a typeface named Perpetua, designed by the British artist Eric Gill (1882–1940) and cut by the Monotype Corporation of London in 1928–30. Perpetua is a contemporary letter of original design, without any direct historical antecedents. The shapes of the roman letters basically derive from stonecutting, a form of lettering in which Gill was eminent. The italic is essentially an inclined roman. The general effect of the typeface in reading sizes is one of lightness and grace. The larger display sizes of the type are extremely elegant and form what is probably the most distinguished series of inscriptional letters cut in the present century.

COMPOSED BY

*Stratford Publishing Services, Brattleboro, Vermont*

PRINTED AND BOUND BY

*Thomson-Shore, Inc., Dexter, Michigan*

DESIGNED BY

*Iris Weinstein*